ROOM 6

SQUEAK!
GOES CLIMBING IN YOSEMITE NATIONAL PARK

by D. Scott Borden • illustrated by Mallory Logan

*Climbing can be extremely dangerous. This book is not meant to provide information on safety.
Please seek the aid of a professional before attempting to climb on your own.

"Now lay down little ones," says Grandma Mouse.

"I want to tell you a bedtime story. This story is about how you can do anything you put your mind to."

In a land of towering rocky cliffs, magnificent waterfalls, and giant trees lives a mouse named Squeak. Squeak lives an average mousey life. She's shy and timid and isn't the toughest or boldest mouse. In fact, she is just like you and me.

Life is pretty ordinary for our little friend Squeak, that is, until one day....

On this day, Squeak is enjoying her meadow home, which is visited by millions of people each year who stare in amazement at a magnificent 3,300-foot tall rock called El Capitan.

Sadly, one of those visitors is so amazed by those cliffs that he stumbles backwards and steps right on poor little Squeak's tail!

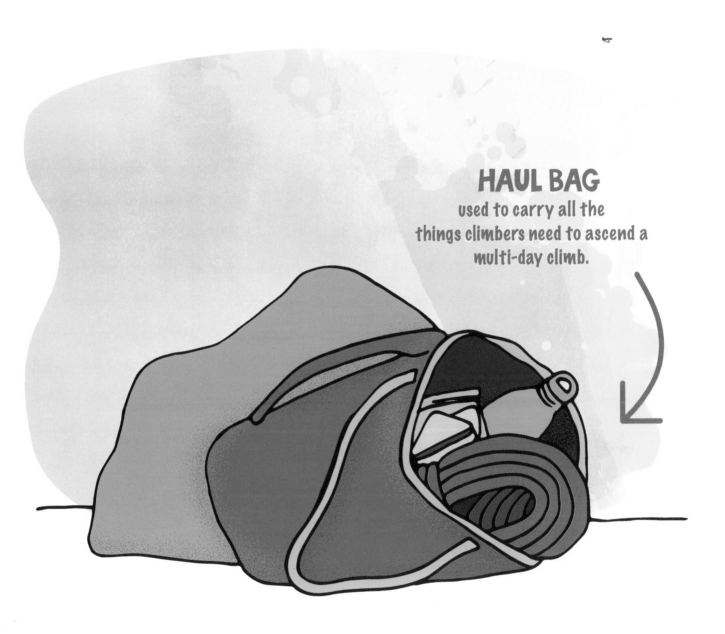

HAUL BAG
used to carry all the things climbers need to ascend a multi-day climb.

Rock climbers also come from around the world to scale El Capitan but most are unsuccessful. Squeak doesn't know, nor care, about this as her tail is in too much pain.

In fact, she is so distracted that she steps right into a climber's **HAUL BAG.**

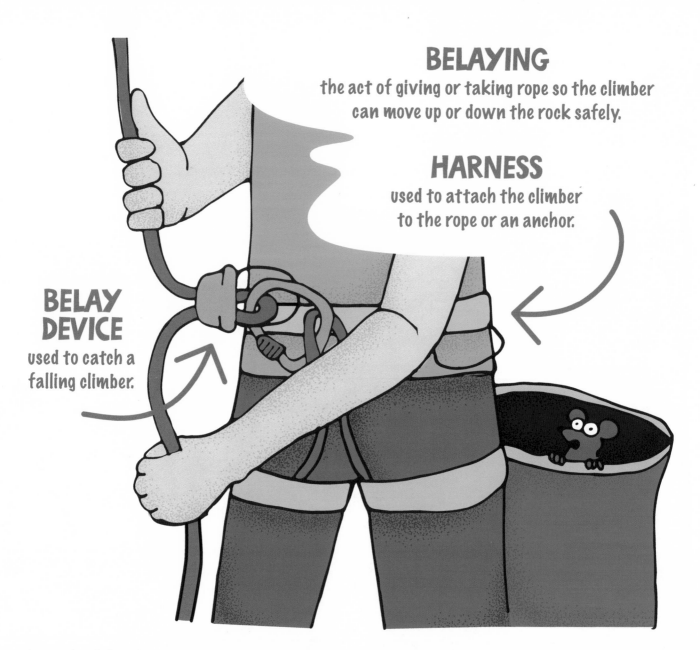

BELAYING
the act of giving or taking rope so the climber
can move up or down the rock safely.

HARNESS
used to attach the climber
to the rope or an anchor.

**BELAY
DEVICE**
used to catch a
falling climber.

Startled by her new surroundings, Squeak peeks her head out and sees Black Bear.

"Help, what is happening?" She yells.

"Don't worry, you're in a **HAUL BAG** and those rock climbers are **BELAYING** each other to keep safe on their journey up El Capitan. See the **BELAY DEVICE** on that **HARNESS?**" Black Bear responds.

But Squeak is too afraid to look, and she sinks back into the **HAUL BAG** and covers her eyes.

"I just can't do it!" She cries.

HELMET
used to protect a
climbers head.

Soon Squeak is high up on El Capitan and feeling very scared when she sees Peregrine Falcon.

"Excuse me? Where am I going?" Squeak asks.

Peregrine Falcon, shocked to see the mouse, swiftly states, **"To the top! It should take you about three days, unless of course you can fly like me. Now don't forget your HELMET!"**

A panicked Squeak cries, "I just can't do it!"

PORTALEDGE
is a bed-like structure attached to an anchor
for sleeping in high, steep places.

Once the sun has gone down Squeak stops worrying. She settles down and explores the **PORTALEDGE,** which is attached to an **ANCHOR.** While the climbers sleep, Squeak enjoys the beautiful stars above.

Waking on the second day, Squeak pokes her head out of the **HAUL BAG** where she sees Blue Belly Lizard.

"Wow, how do you just stand on the vertical rock like that?" Squeak asks.

Blue Belly Lizard does two quick pushups and proudly responds, **"Well, unlike CLIMBING SHOES with sticky rubber, I have small hairs on the bottoms of my feet that help me climb."**

Squeak is too scared to climb like Lizard. She just wants this whole experience to be over. But before she can ask Lizard more questions a loud yell from above interrupts, **"Faaaallllliiiinnnngggg!"**

The climber has had a safe fall thanks to some good **BELAYING** and no one is injured.

Squeak curiously pokes her head out of the **HAUL BAG** where she see Pacific Tree Frog. Squeak is so excited, she explains her whole story of being dragged up the rock and meeting the other animals.

Tree Frog listens and then asks, **"Why didn't you just climb down?"**

"Because I don't know how," Squeak whimpers.

"Well, have you ever tried?" Tree Frog replies.

"I just can't do it!" Squeak cries.

It's now the third day and Squeak is feeling very homesick for her meadow home. Looking up, she can see the top of El Capitan not far above.

Suddenly Squeak hears the climbers frantically yelling.

THE ROPE IS STUCK!

I CAN'T FREE IT!

Squeak's heart sinks. The climbers continue to shout back and forth for what feels like hours, and Squeak knows they're trapped.

Squeak desperately wants to help, but how?

She doesn't know anything about belaying like Black Bear.

She can't fly like Peregrine Falcon.

She can't climb like Blue Belly Lizard or Pacific Tree Frog.

She is utterly helpless.

Or is she?

At that moment Squeak musters up all of her courage and steps out of the **HAUL BAG**.

Placing one foot in front of the other, she slowly climbs to where the rope is stuck.

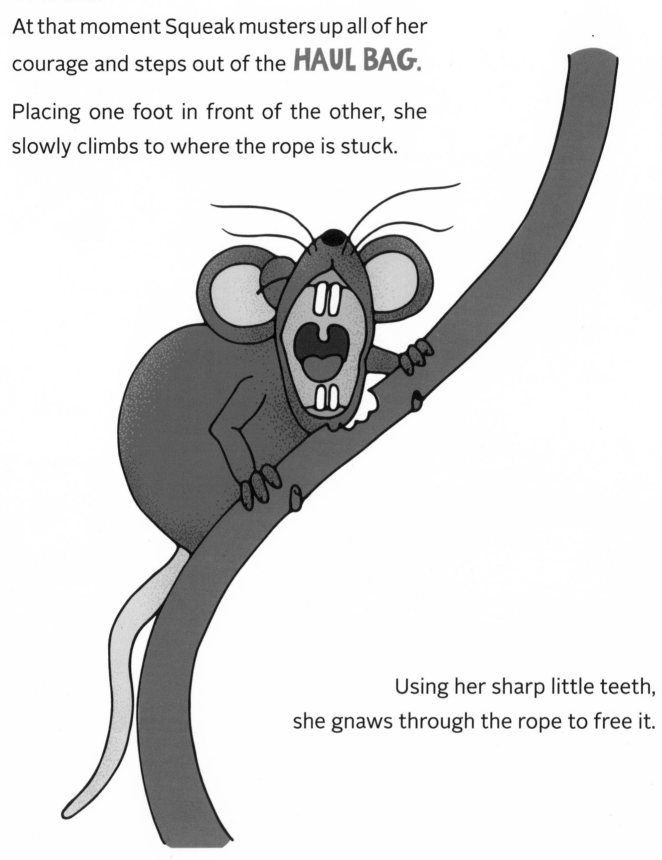

Using her sharp little teeth, she gnaws through the rope to free it.

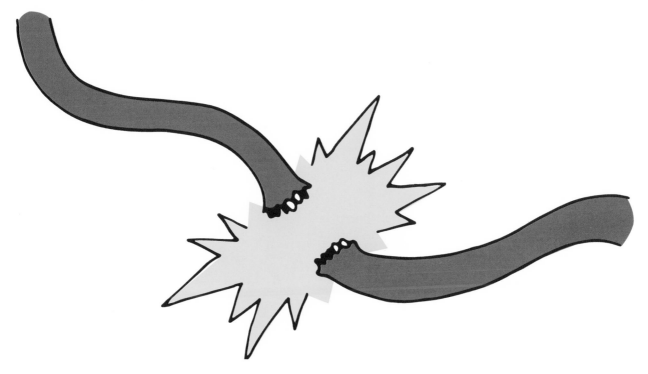

Right as she chews the last thread, the climbers pull the rope free and yell, **"Hooooray!"**

Squeak saved the day!

With a burst of courage and pride she climbs to the top of El Capitan on her own, where she joins the climbers in celebrating their success.

It is truly a wonderful feeling for everyone!
Standing there on top of El Capitan, Squeak feels bigger than ever

Maybe, just maybe, she will even look for another **HAUL BAG** and try to help new climbers reach their dreams of scaling the magnificent cliffs of El Capitan.

The young mice have all fallen asleep, except one.

"Grandma?" The little mouse asks.

"Yes little one?" Grandma Mouse replies.

"Is that a real story?"

GRANDMA SQUEAK

"It IS little one. I was Squeak as a young mouse. And maybe, just maybe, you too will learn to climb someday. Because, just like me, you too can do it."

GLOSSARY

ANCHOR
attaches a climber to a surface for safety.

BELAY DEVICE
catches a falling climber.
BELAYING
giving or taking rope so the climber can
move up or down the rock safely.

CLIMBING SHOES
shoes with sticky rubber that make it easier
to climb.

HARNESS
attaches the climber to the rope or an anchor.

HAUL BAG
carries all the things climbers need to ascend
a multi-day climb.

HELMET
protects a climbers head.

PORTALEDGE
a bed-like structure attached to an anchor
for sleeping on.

(BRIEF) HISTORY OF EL CAPITAN CLIMBING

1957: Warren Harding & Team Make First Aid Ascent

1993: Lynn Hill First Free Climb of "The Nose"

2012: Hans Florine and Alex Honnold Climb in Only 2 hours and 23 minutes

2017: Alex Honnold First Ascent Without a Rope

*Climbing can be extremely dangerous. This book is not meant to provide information on safety.
Please seek the aid of a professional before attempting to climb on your own.

Protect America's Climbing

A portion of each purchase of **SQUEAK!**
benefits the Access Fund and is generously matched by:

Squeak! is brought to you by

THE CLIMBING ZINE

Luke Mehall
Snail Mail: P.O. Box 673 / Durango, CO 81302
Telephone: 970/376-3116
Website: climbingzine.com